W9-BPN-778

Art's
Alive!

What are Textiles?

Ruth Thomson

SEA-TO-SEA
Mankato Collingwood London

This edition first published in 2006 by
Sea-to-Sea Publications
1980 Lookout Drive
North Mankato
Minnesota 56003

Printed in China

Library of Congress Cataloging-in-Publication Data:

Thomson, Ruth, 1949-
    What are textiles? / Ruth Thomson.
        p. cm. − (Art's alive!)
    ISBN 1-932889-90-6
    1. Hand weaving−Juvenile literature. 2. Textile fabrics−Juvenile literature. I. Title. II.
    Art's alive (North Mankato, Minn.)

TT848.T427 2005
746−dc22

                                                            2004062735

9 8 7 6 5 4 3 2

Published by arrangement with the Watts Publishing Group Ltd, London

Editor: Caryn Jenner
Design: Sphere Design
Art director: Jonathan Hair
Picture research: Diana Morris
Art consultant: Janet Pope

The publisher wishes to thank Fiona Cole for her assistance with the artwork and activities in this book.
Thanks also to Florence McLaughlin and Heather Webster.

All photographs taken by Ray Moller unless otherwise credited.

Acknowledgments:
With special authorization of the City of Bayeux/Bridgeman Art Library: 17. Dinodia: 19. DPA/The Image
Works/Topham: 22tl. Pascal Goetgheluck/SPL: 9br. Historical Picture Archive/Corbis: 23. Jeremy
Horner/Corbis: 15. Wolfgang Kaehler/Corbis: 21. Kelley-Mooney Photography/Corbis: 13. Lawrence
Manning/Corbis: 10cr. Philadelphia Museum of Art/Corbis: front cover, 25. Anders Ryman/Corbis: 10cl.
Joseph Sohm, ChromoSohm Inc./Corbis: 9tl. Adam Woolfitt/Corbis: 8bl.

Every attempt has been made to clear copyright. Should there be any inadvertent omission please apply to the
publisher for rectification.

Contents

What are textiles?

Textiles are made from **fibers**. Other words for textiles are cloth, material, and fabric.

Clothes ▷
Clothes are made from soft, comfortable textiles. They trap air to keep us warm.

◁ Towels
Some textiles soak up water easily. We use them to dry ourselves after a wash or bath.

Bags ▷
Some textiles are tough and waterproof. They are perfect for making knapsacks.

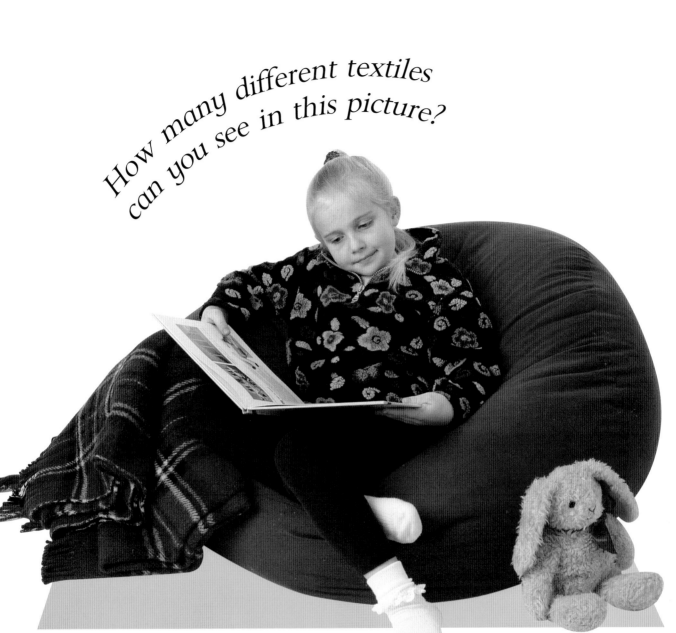

How many different textiles can you see in this picture?

A textile hunt
Look around your home to see how many different textiles you can find. Search in the bathroom and kitchen, and in cupboards and drawers.

What are textiles made from?

Some textiles, such as wool, cotton, and silk, are made from **natural** fibers.

Wool

Wool comes from sheep. Farmers clip the wool off the sheep. The sheep will soon grow more!

Wool keeps you warm.

What does it feel like?
Feel some textiles. What are they like? Use these words to help describe them.

soft   warm   scratchy
rough   heavy   light
slippery   smooth   fluffy

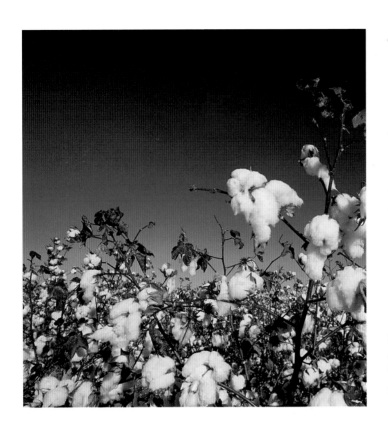

Cotton

Cotton comes from the seed-hairs of a plant. The seed pods are called bolls. Each one has thousands of hairs.

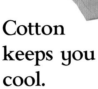

Cotton keeps you cool.

Silk

Silk comes from the cocoons of silkworms. Workers unravel long silk threads from the cocoons and twist them together.

Silk is soft and light.

9

Making yarn

The fibers of wool or cotton are twisted together into long lengths of **yarn**.
This is called spinning.

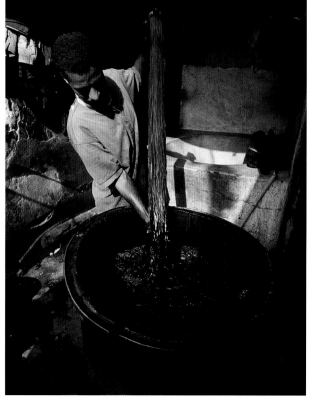

▲ Hand-spinning
This woman twirls a **spindle** and pulls the wool. The fibers lengthen and twist together to make yarn.

▲ Hand-dyeing
Dye gives the yarn color. Here, yarn is being colored in a pot of blue dye.

Look at the labels inside your clothes to see what they are made of.

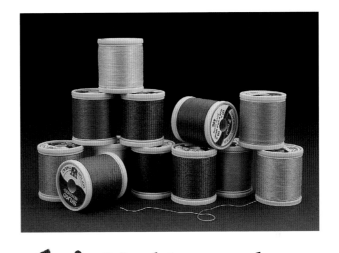

▲ **Machine-made**
Most wool and thread is spun and dyed in factories called mills. Mills also make yarns that are not natural, such as viscose and acrylic.

▲ **Knitting wool**
Wool like this is often used for knitting.

Twisting yarn
Roll a piece of cotton batting between your hands. See how the fibers lengthen as you twist them together.

Weaving

Cloth is made by criss-crossing threads over and under each other on a frame called a **loom**. This is known as weaving.

Warp and weft ▶

Look at some woven cloth. Threads that go up and down are called the warp. Threads that go across are called the weft.

Weaving with paper

warp — — weft

1
Lay paper strips on thin cardboard, leaving spaces in between. Glue both ends onto the card.

2
Cut more strips in other colors. Weave one strip over and under the warp strips.

3
Weave the next strip *under* and then *over*. Repeat steps 2 and 3 until your weaving is complete.

12

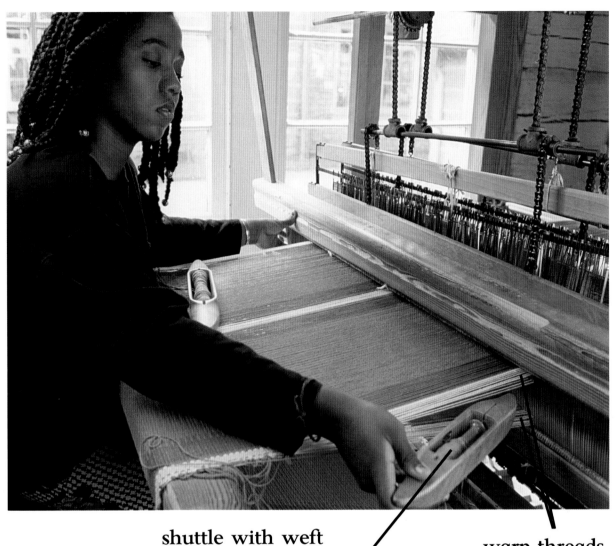

shuttle with weft
thread wound inside

warp threads

▲ Weaving

This woman is weaving on a big
wooden loom. She is about to put the
shuttle through the warp threads to
make the criss-crossing weft threads.

Weaving patterns

Textiles with colored **patterns** are made when the warp and weft threads are different colors.

Going dotty
Design a pattern for a T-shirt. You can choose one repeating shape, like this, or use a few different ones.

🔺 **Patterned cloth**
Patterns on modern looms are computer-controlled. The patterns can be very simple or very complicated.

What three animals can you see in the pattern of this textile?

▲ **Tarabuco weaving from South America**

This textile was woven by hand. The weaver used several shuttles, each with a different color of thread, to make these patterns.

Embroidery

Embroidery is a way of decorating textiles with stitched patterns or pictures.

Fancy fish ▶
This embroidery was made with smooth, silky threads.

A thread picture
Draw an outline picture on thin cardboard. Glue some embroidery threads over the outlines.

A glittery bag ▲
Sequins and beads can be added to embroideries.

▲ The Bayeux Tapestry

This long, woolen embroidery was made more than 900 years ago. It tells the story of how William the Conqueror and his men sailed from France to England, and won the Battle of Hastings in 1066.

Tie-dye

If some parts of a textile are tied before it is dyed, these parts do not change color.

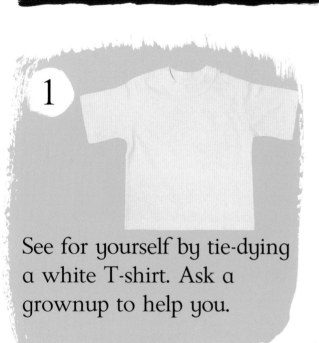

1 See for yourself by tie-dying a white T-shirt. Ask a grownup to help you.

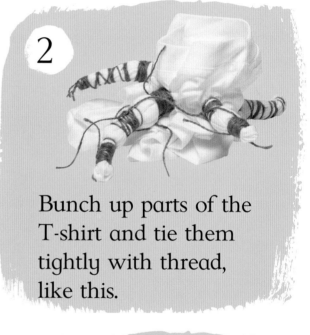

2 Bunch up parts of the T-shirt and tie them tightly with thread, like this.

3 Ask a grown-up to soak the T-shirt in dye. Rinse it well and leave it to dry.

4 Untie the threads. The T-shirt will have white patches where it was tied.

▲ Tie-dyed cloth from India

Look how many bunches have been tied
in this textile. The cloth has been dyed,
but the threads have not yet been untied.

Batik

To make batik, people draw patterns on textiles using a pen of hot wax. Then they dye the textiles. The dye does not stick to wax.

Hand-drawn patterns
When the wax is removed, the pattern shows up on the undyed cloth.

Close-up of batik pattern

A waxy picture
Using wax crayons, draw a pattern on some paper. Paint over it with watery paint. The wax marks will show through the paint.

▲ Fish batik from Indonesia

This batik was waxed and dyed many times, starting with the lightest color and ending with the darkest. Some colors are mixed together to make new colors.

Look carefully at this batik. In what order do you think the colors were dyed?

Block printing

Another way to make patterns on textiles is by printing with wood blocks.

▲ Repeating patterns

The printer presses an inky block onto cloth again and again to make a pattern.

carved
wood blocks

sponge blocks

Sponge prints

Cut some sponges into shapes. Dip them in paint. Press them onto paper to make a printed picture.

What animals can you see
hiding among the plants?

▲ **Brother Rabbit print,
William Morris, 1882**

This cloth is printed with a pattern
of leaves, flowers, and animals.

Patchwork

Patchwork is usually made from many pieces of cloth of all different colors.

◀ Patchwork pieces

Long ago, women saved scraps left over from making dresses. They cut these into shapes and sewed them together to make patchwork **quilts** like this one.

Common patchwork shapes

square   diamond   hexagon

Patchwork patterns

Carefully color squared paper to make lots of different patchwork patterns.

Can you see what shape has been used to make this starry quilt?

🔺 Patchwork quilt,
Rebecca Scattergood Savery, 1839

A patchwork quilt like this takes a long time to make. Sometimes, a group of people get together to sew a quilt. This is called a quilting bee.

Appliqué

Appliqué pictures have layers of fabric.
The layers are stitched one on top of the other.

◀ **Crazy cats**

This picture has many layers of fabric. The black layer is on top. It has been cut away to let the other colors show through.

A whale of a time
Make your own appliqué picture. Cut fabric shapes and glue them to a piece of thin cardboard.

How many different animals, birds, and insects can you find below?

▼ **Appliqué from Colombia**

This colorful appliqué shows everyday country life in Colombia, South America. What are all the people doing?

Quiz

1. Find three things in the book that are made from textiles and can be used to carry things.

2. Does wool come from a plant or an animal?

3. Has this T-shirt been dyed or printed?

4. What is this used for?

5. What is the name for textiles made with layers of cloth?

Glossary

dye A dye is used to change the color of textiles. The textiles are usually soaked or dipped in dye.

fiber A very thin thread. Fibers are twisted together to make yarn.

loom A machine used to weave yarn into cloth.

natural Found in nature. Wool, cotton, and silk are examples of natural textiles.

pattern A repeated design.

quilt A cover for a bed. Quilts are often made with patchwork.

shuttle A tool used with a weaving loom. The shuttle holds the weft thread as it criss-crosses with the warp threads to make cloth.

spindle A thin rod used to spin yarn.

yarn Thread used for making cloth. Yarn is made from fibers such as wool, cotton, or silk.

Websites

www.crayola.com
A colorful site with lots of fabric craft ideas and activities.

www.bayeuxtapestry.org.uk
An explanation of the story depicted in the Bayeux Tapestry and information on the history of the Tapestry itself.

www.americanhistory.si.edu/quilts/
Pictures of all sorts of quilts, including patchwork, appliqué, and embroidery.

www.morrissociety.org
A website about the life and work of William Morris, with pictures of his designs for tapestries and textiles.

Note to parents and teachers
Every effort has been made by the Publishers to ensure that these websites are suitable for children. However, because of the nature of the Internet, it is impossible to guarantee that the contents of these sites will not be altered. We strongly advise that Internet access is supervised by a responsible adult.

Index